HARVESTING SOLAR, WIND AND TIDAL POWER

ENVIRONMENT FOR KIDS
CHILDREN'S EARTH SCIENCE BOOKS

Speedy Publishing LLC
40 E. Main St. #1156
Newark, DE 19711
www.speedypublishing.com
Copyright 2017

All Rights reserved. No part of this book may be reproduced or used in any way or form or by any means whether electronic or mechanical, this means that you cannot record or photocopy any material ideas or tips that are provided in this book.

In this book, we're going to talk about the different types of renewable energy. So, let's get right to it!

Scientists and environmentalists are very concerned about the amount of pollution that human populations are producing. As the number of people on Earth increases, we're using more and more sources of energy to heat our homes and to power our buildings and factories.

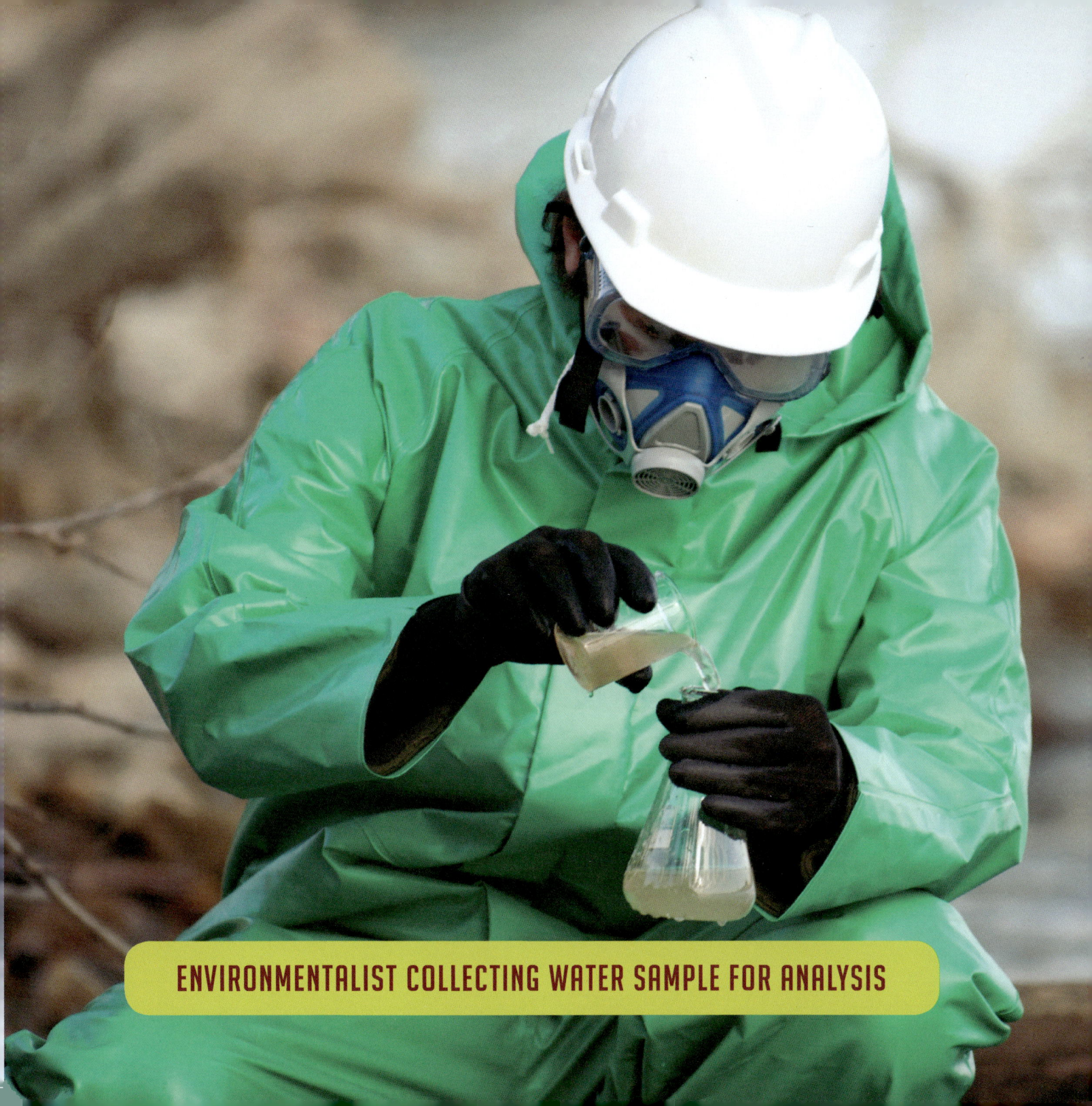
ENVIRONMENTALIST COLLECTING WATER SAMPLE FOR ANALYSIS

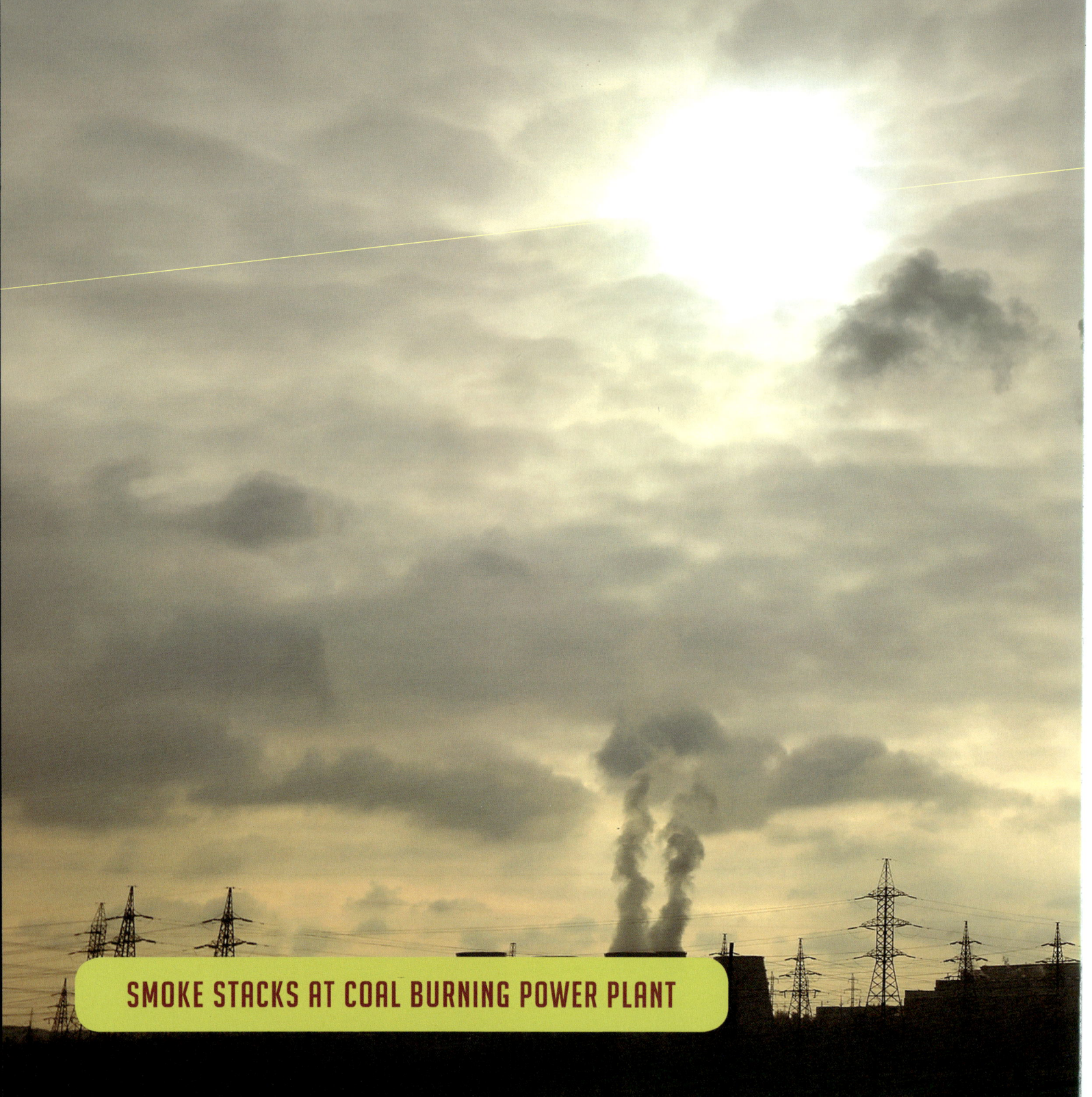
SMOKE STACKS AT COAL BURNING POWER PLANT

Since the Industrial Age, we've been using vast amounts of petroleum, coal, and natural gas for our energy sources. These sources of energy are fossil fuels and they are non-renewable.

THE DIFFERENCE BETWEEN NON-RENEWABLE AND RENEWABLE ENERGY

It took millions of years for non-renewable energy sources to form deep within the Earth. Once we use them up, there will be no further resources to tap. An even larger problem than the fact that these fuels are in limited supply is the dangerous, toxic pollution they emit.

TOXIC POLLUTION

Renewable energy sources, such as wind power, energy from the sun, and tidal energy, have been used for many centuries. These sources are considered renewable because they don't get "used up."

For example, the sun will continue to send warmth to the Earth for billions of years, so solar power is a renewable energy source. However, it's only been in the last few decades that there has been more of an interest in making renewable energy sources the major way that we get our energy.

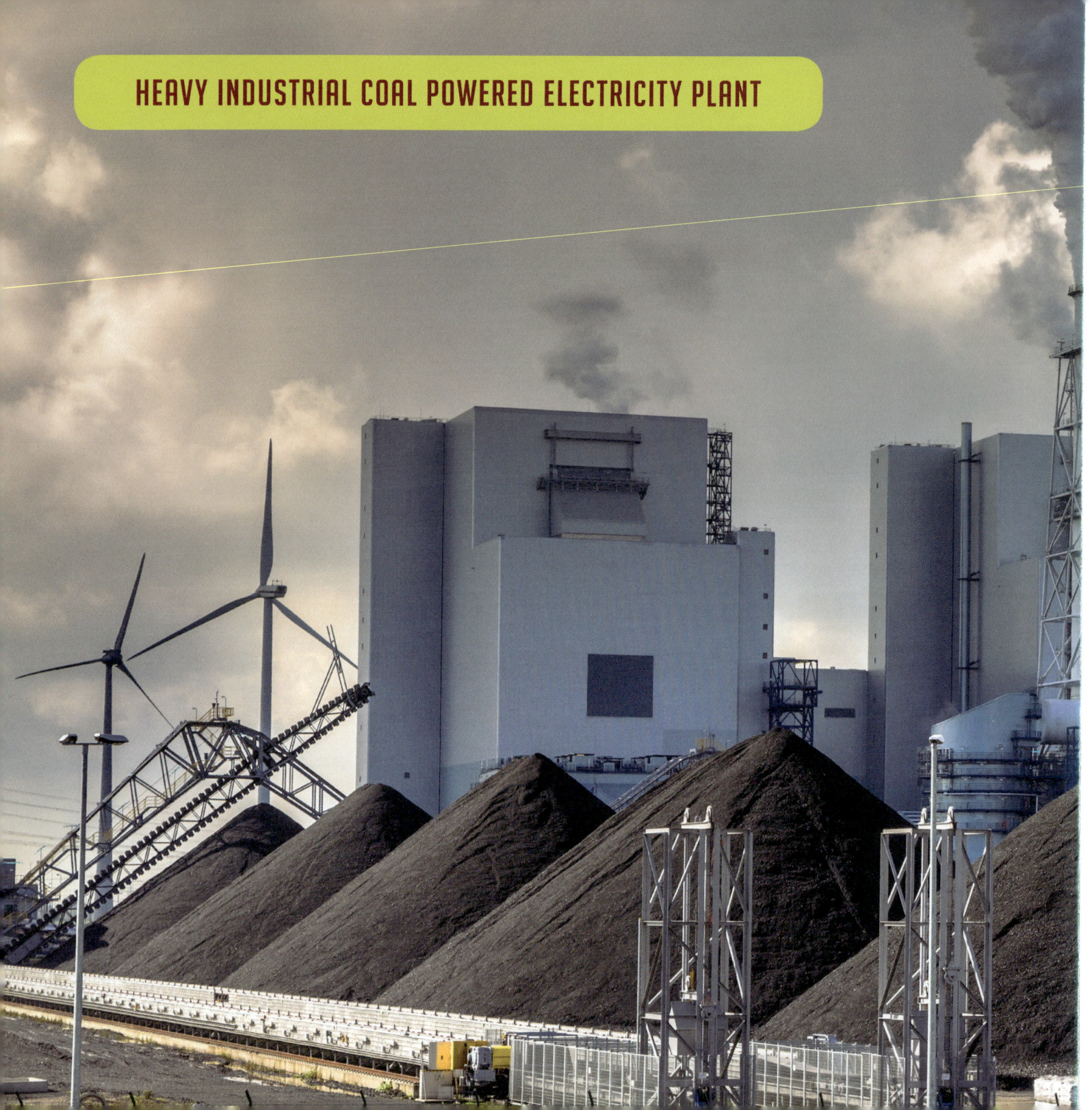

WHAT TYPES OF ENERGY ARE BEING USED TODAY?

Today, there are numerous sources of energy being used around the world, but non-renewable energy is still the major source. Here are the percentages:

- Oil, which is non-renewable, 33%
- Coal, which is non-renewable, 29%

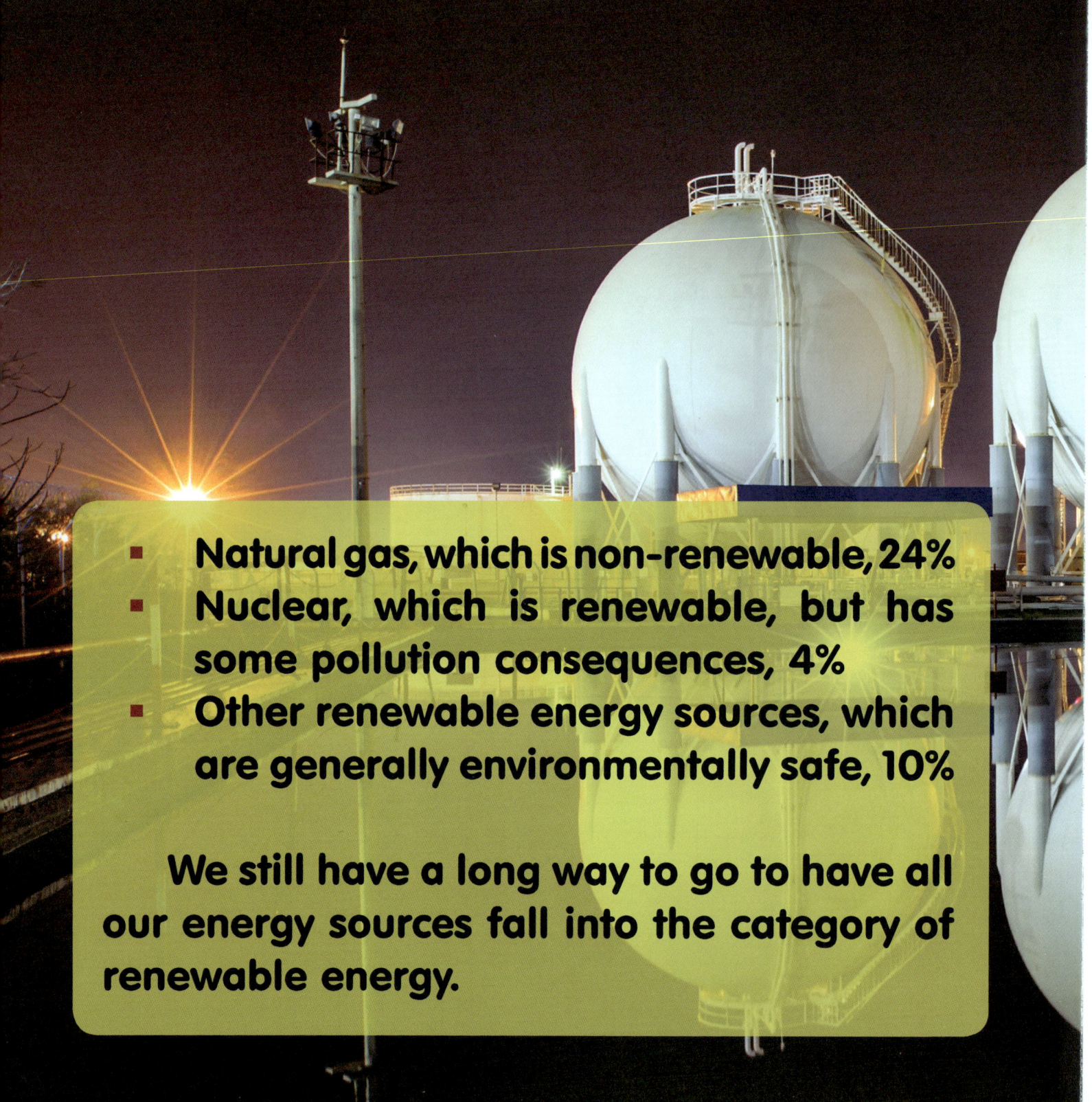

- Natural gas, which is non-renewable, 24%
- Nuclear, which is renewable, but has some pollution consequences, 4%
- Other renewable energy sources, which are generally environmentally safe, 10%

We still have a long way to go to have all our energy sources fall into the category of renewable energy.

THE DIFFERENT TYPES OF RENEWABLE ENERGY

Today, around the world, about 10% of the energy sources used are renewable sources. Scientists and governments are actively looking for new ways to convert these resources into inexpensive, reliable methods for obtaining energy.

DAM OF HYDROELECTRIC POWER PLANT

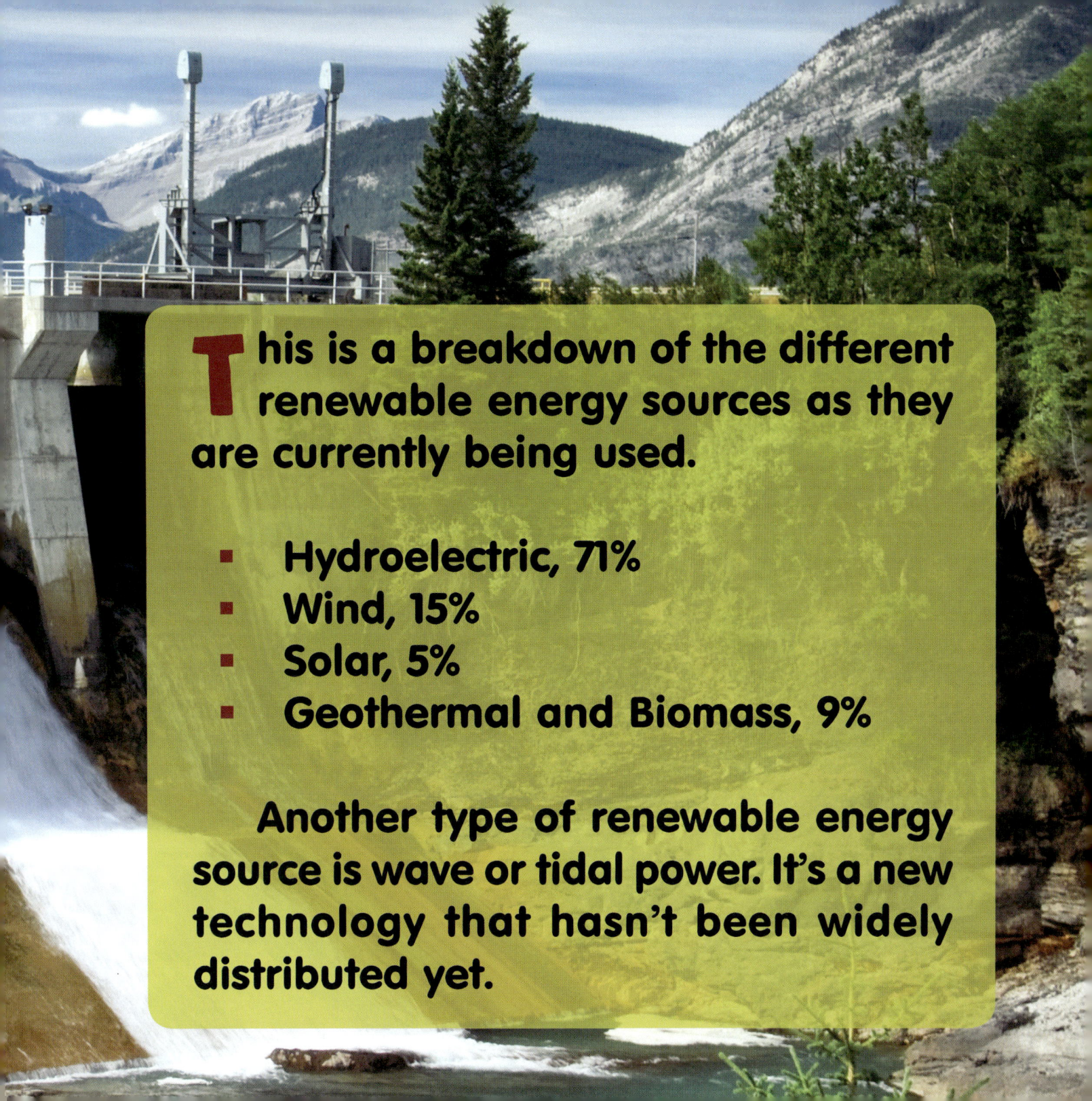

This is a breakdown of the different renewable energy sources as they are currently being used.

- Hydroelectric, 71%
- Wind, 15%
- Solar, 5%
- Geothermal and Biomass, 9%

Another type of renewable energy source is wave or tidal power. It's a new technology that hasn't been widely distributed yet.

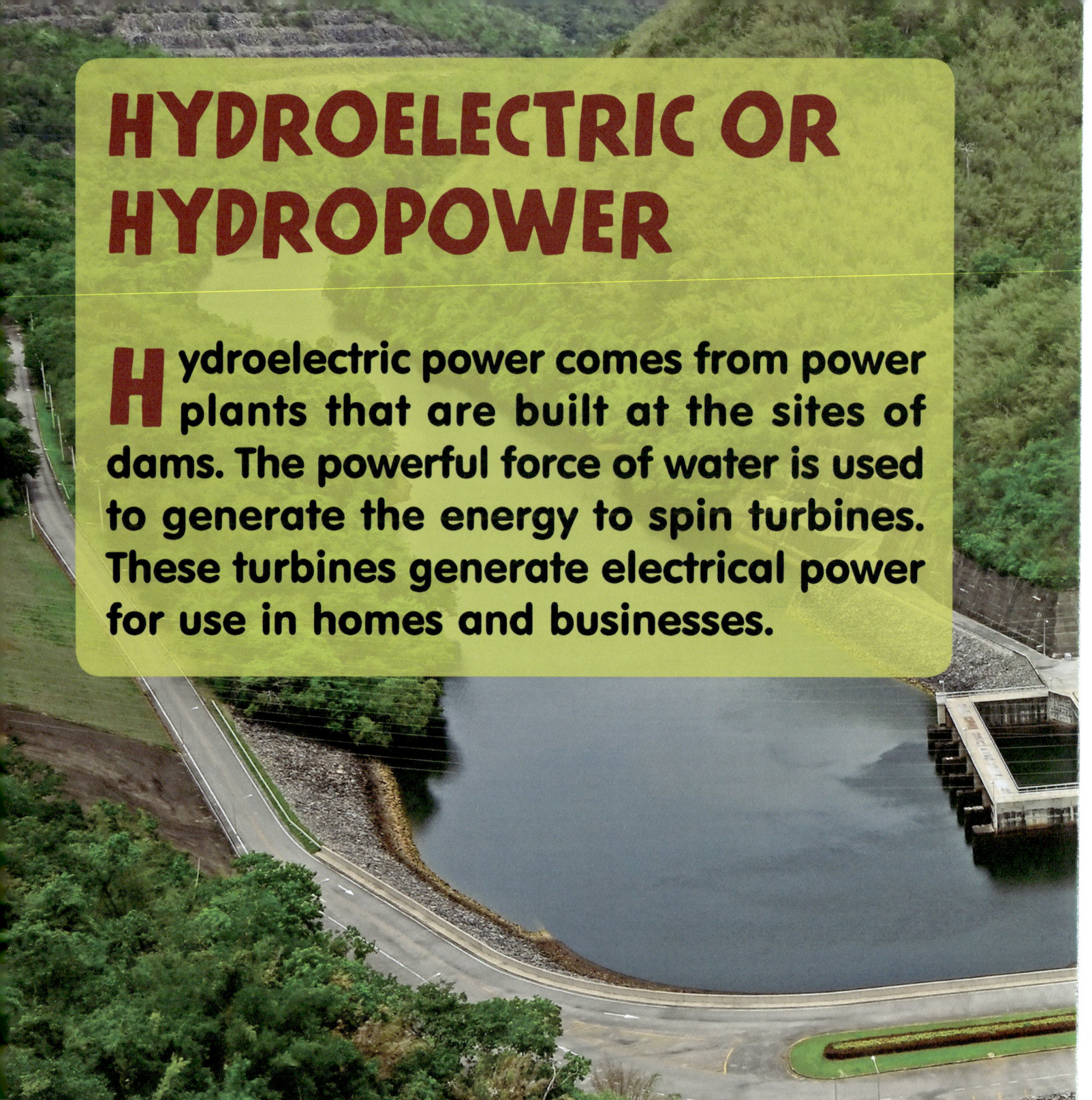

HYDROELECTRIC OR HYDROPOWER

Hydroelectric power comes from power plants that are built at the sites of dams. The powerful force of water is used to generate the energy to spin turbines. These turbines generate electrical power for use in homes and businesses.

WATER PLANT POWER DAM ENERGY

WIND POWER

Windmills have been around for many centuries. Wind turbines are the more modern form of this type of energy. The wind's power spins the turbines and they in turn create electricity.

WIND TURBINES

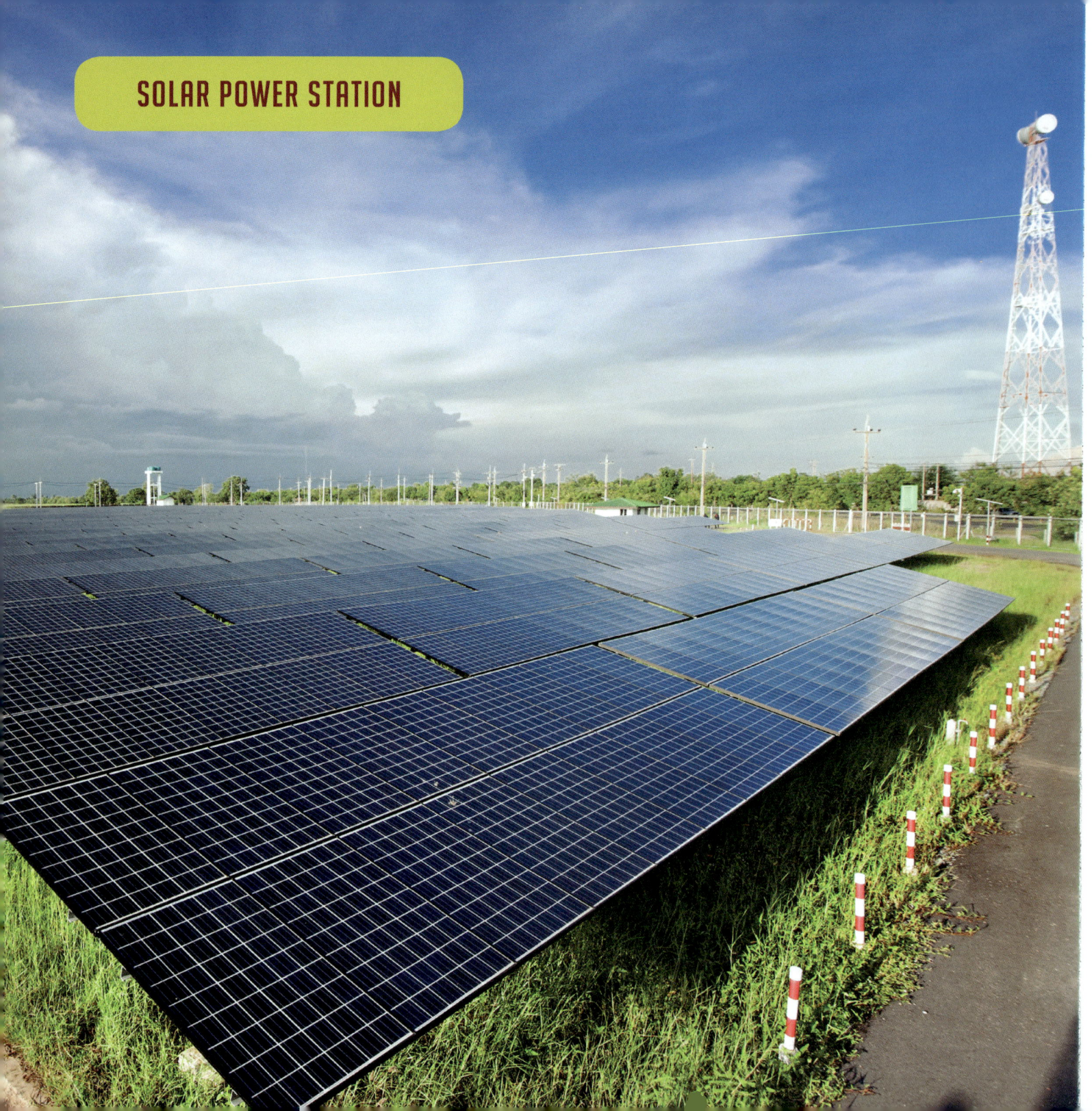

SOLAR POWER

The sun's rays can heat buildings or pools. Through the use of solar cells, the rays of the sun can also be converted to electricity. If there were a way to harness all the sunlight that travels to Earth in just one hour, there would be enough energy for the world's needs for an entire year!

GEOTHERMAL ENERGY

The Earth's core has a tremendous amount of heat. This heat can be converted into an energy source used for heating the interiors of homes and office buildings. Steam from underground can be converted to electrical energy.

GEOTHERMAL POWER STATION

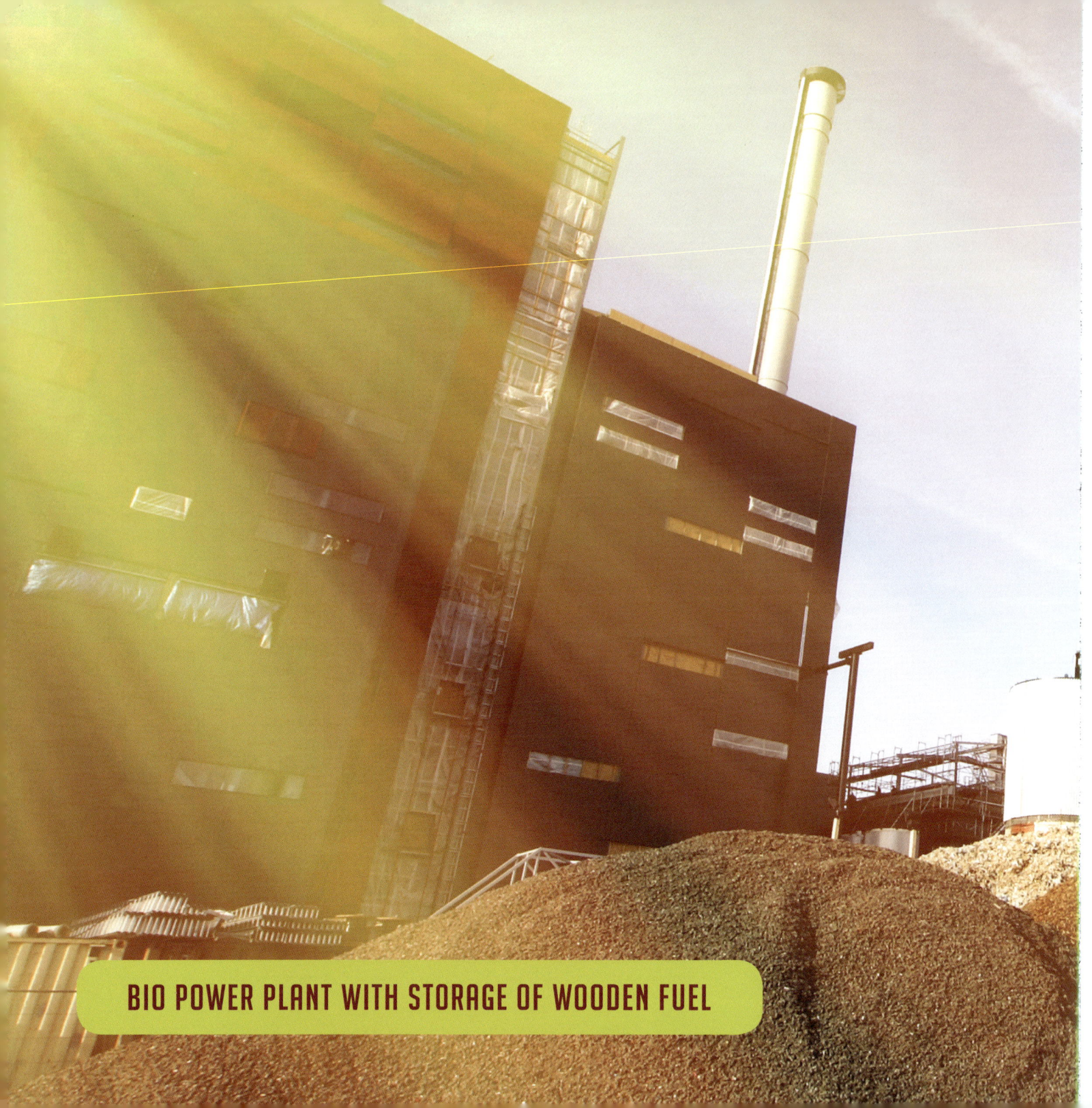

BIOMASS ENERGY

Plants have their own process to harness energy from the sun. This process is called photosynthesis. The energy locked inside plants can be converted by burning wood from trees. It's also possible to make fuel from corn and other types of plants. These types of fuels, from organic materials, are called biodiesel and ethanol. Even methane gas that comes from decaying trash and manure can be used to make energy.

WAVE AND TIDAL POWER

The Earth has five oceans. These oceans have a tremendous amount of energy in their moving waves as well as their day-to-day tides. Scientists are developing new ways to harness this energy.

Let's look at the ways that three of these forms of renewable energy work, and their advantages and disadvantages.

TIDE MILL LOCATED ON THE EDGE OF A SEA

SOLAR CELL

HOW DOES SOLAR POWER WORK?

There are two basic ways that energy from the sun gets converted into useable energy for our purposes: solar cells and solar panels.

Solar cells are sometimes described as photovoltaic cells. Yet another name for them is PV devices. Solar cells transform the energy that comes from light to electricity. There are alloys of silicon and other materials within these cells and they come in all sizes. Some are so small they are used within calculators or phones.

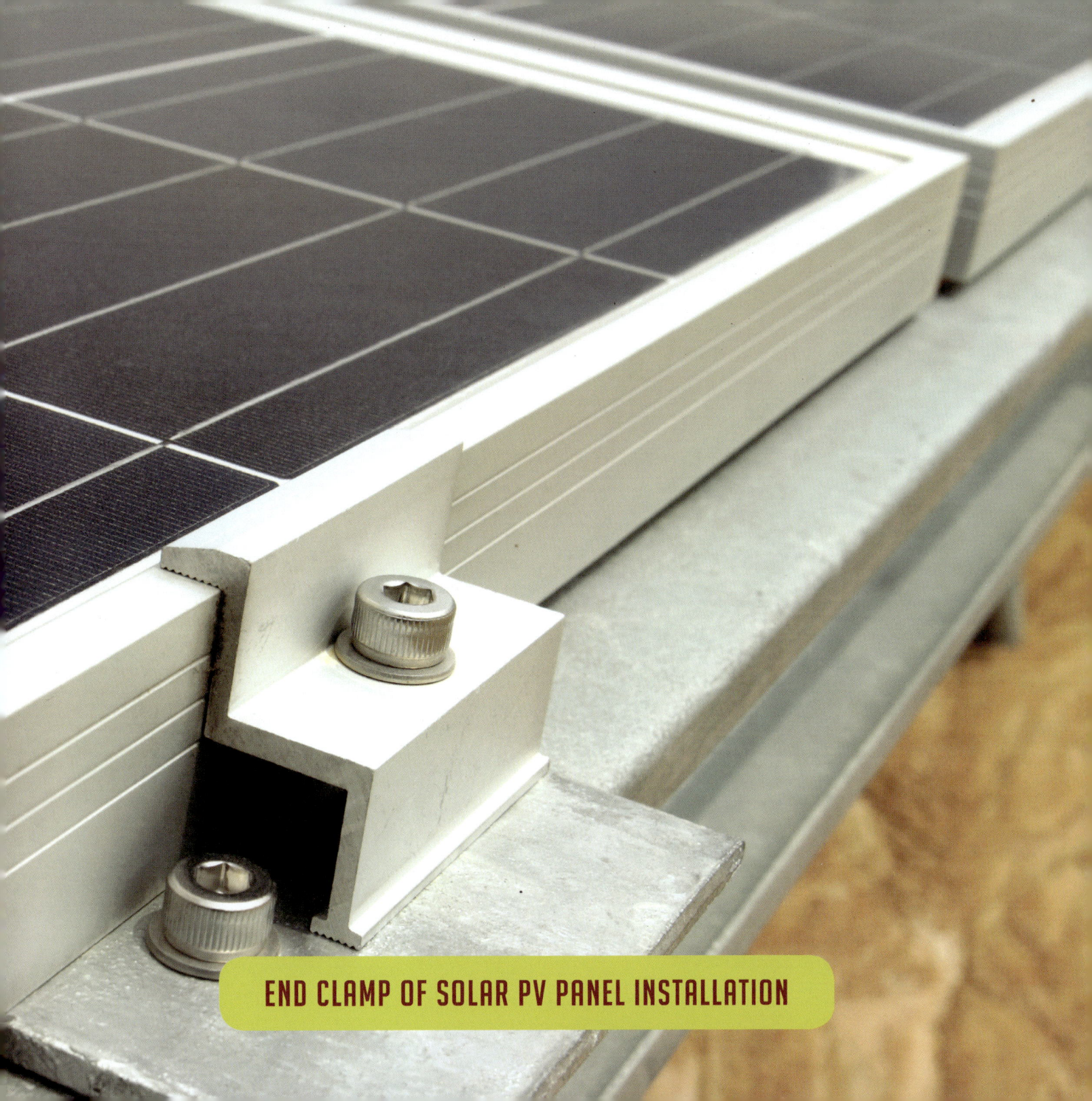

END CLAMP OF SOLAR PV PANEL INSTALLATION

Huge arrays of PV devices can power signs that are used for road directions. Some arrays are even used to give power to satellites that rotate around the Earth.

Solar panels also gather the sun's rays, but instead of creating electricity, they heat water directly. Cold water from a storage tank is pumped into the solar panel. Once the sun heats the water up, it goes back to the tank to heat a swimming pool or a building. These types of panels are usually located on rooftops so they can get the most sunlight.

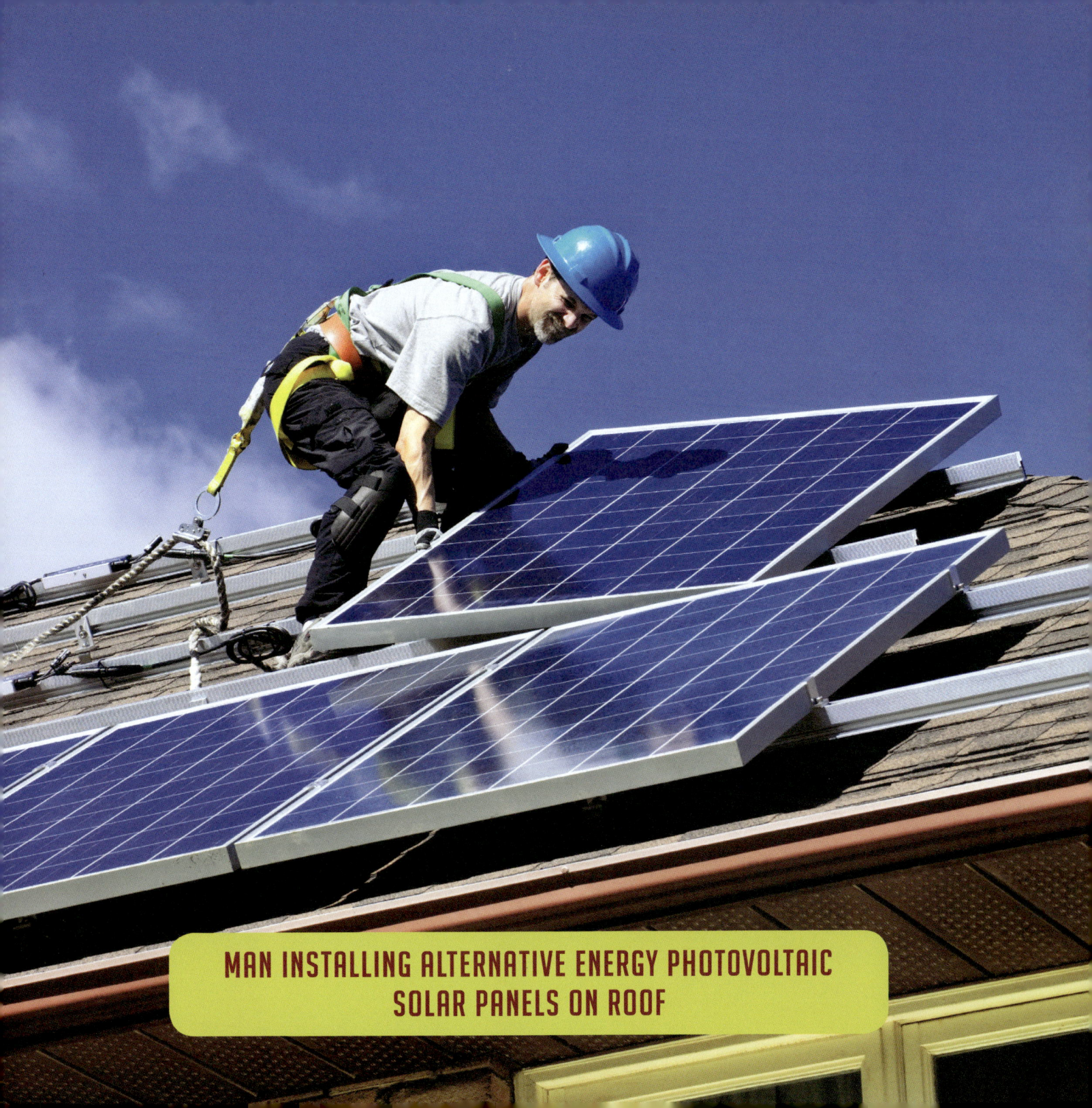

MAN INSTALLING ALTERNATIVE ENERGY PHOTOVOLTAIC SOLAR PANELS ON ROOF

SUN RAYS

ADVANTAGES

Gathering the sun's energy through solar panels and cells doesn't emit smoke, carbon dioxide, or other harmful air pollutants.

DISADVANTAGES

Even though the sun is always there, sometimes bad weather causes the sun's rays to be diminished. At night, we're turned away from the sun, so we can't capture the sun's energy during that time. Even though there's almost unlimited power available from the sun's rays, these are the reasons we can't be completely dependent on the sun for our energy.

HOW DOES WIND POWER WORK?

When it's a sunny day, the atmosphere over the land heats up more quickly than the atmosphere over water. The heated air begins to rise. The colder air over the water is denser than the heated air so it falls in altitude and gradually replaces the air that was positioned over the land.

At night, the opposite happens. The air that is traveling over the water is warmer and it gradually rises and is replaced by the colder air that's now positioned over the land. It's this cycle that keeps the air moving and creating wind.

The wind has a lot of stored energy called kinetic energy. The wind moves the blades of the wind turbine. The blades make a shaft spin. The shaft is connected to a generator, which creates electrical power.

The electricity flows through lines for transmission and is then distributed to substations. From the substations, it goes to power homes, schools, and businesses.

ADVANTAGES

Wind energy doesn't produce any type of toxic pollution or emission.

DISADVANTAGES

Sometimes the wind isn't powerful enough to spin the turbines. A wind speed of about 14 miles per hour is necessary to transform the energy of the wind into electrical power. Wind turbines can't work in regions where the wind is very turbulent or high speed. It's been shown that wind turbines sometimes kill birds in flight. Scientists are working to find ways of eliminating this disadvantage.

WATER RESERVOIR

HOW DOES TIDAL POWER WORK?

Scientists are working on three different ways to harness the power of the tides: surface devices, underwater devices, and reservoirs.

Surface devices get power from waves as they move up and then down on the ocean's surfaces. Underwater devices come in various different shapes. Some are similar to balloons in shape and they are attached to the floor of the ocean.

Others are long snakelike tubes that stretch out over the ocean's surface. In both cases, the waves cause movements, which then set a turbine into motion. The turbine creates the energy from the wave movements into electrical energy. A reservoir is located on the coastline. As the waves crash on shore and then go back out to the ocean they are forced to travel down tubes. The power of these waves makes the blades of a turbine turn, which transforms the energy into electrical power.

ADVANTAGES

Tidal power is a renewable energy source that doesn't emit any toxic fumes or other pollutants. Tidal currents are very predictable and have known cycles, unlike wind, which is not as predictable. Tidal power plants have a long lifespan, which makes them cost effective.

DISADVANTAGES

It's not yet clear what environmental effects may occur from manipulating the ocean. The process may have some serious effects like the problems caused by hydroelectric dams. Hydroelectric dams sometimes cause environmental changes due to the alteration in water flow. They can also cause the destruction of fish habitats and spinning turbines sometimes injure schools of fish. Although tidal devices and tidal power plants may be cost effective in the long run, since they are still at the experimental stage they are expensive to construct.

SCHOOL OF FISH

Awesome! Now you know more about Solar, Wind, and Tidal power and their advantages and disadvantages. You can find more Earth Science books from Baby Professor by searching the website of your favorite book retailer.

Printed by Amazon Italia Logistica S.r.l.
Torrazza Piemonte (TO), Italy